Kahn ...

The S.M.A.R.T. *Sista's*
Guide to College

Secrets your parents, guidance counselors,
and campus advisors forgot to tell you!

For My Mother
Barbara L. Kennedy
the Original S.M.A.R.T. Sista

Acknowledgements

Special thanks to: my Father, Grover Kennedy, for your unconditional love and support as I find my way through life; my sister Kanika believing in my dreams and me. Thank you to Autwan for being a true friend even though I can be handful at times. Thank you to the Strong Family (Tyrone, Tameka, Trinity & Tyson) for being an inspiration and a source of love and joy! Lakeysha you are a phenomenal friend and thank you for pushing me even when I wanted to just stop, you are FABULOUS!

Table Of Contents

Introduction

Hello Sistas,

I remember my first day of college. My Dad and I drove to Duke University after dropping off my older sister at school in Texas. We pulled up to the campus with a mini–van full of boxes. I was nervous and excited all at the same time!

After we unloaded and my Dad made his way back home to Detroit, it was time for the adventure to begin. There were orientations, welcome receptions, and a lot of information given to us about what to expect and how to get started. However, looking back there was a WHOLE lot of information that campus advisors and the "official" welcome committee didn't tell me.

I was lucky, I had an older sister who had two years of college under her belt and she shared with me an abundance of great information that made a HUGE difference in my freshman year. In fact, her advice kept me out of a lot of trouble AND helped me take advantage of many of things I may not have tried otherwise.

I started writing this guide as I prepared to send my little cousin's off to college and realized there was a whole lot I needed to share with them before they left.

This book is for all the young ladies who do not have a big sister/cousin to show them the ropes, AND for those who do. Enjoy!

Disclaimer

This book is for educational and entertainment purposes only. The opinions and advice contained within this book are recommendations based on the author's and other contributors personal experiences and are intended to provide helpful information on the areas discussed. Neither the author nor other contributors are engaged in or render any professional, legal, or any other kind of professional advice. Neither the publisher nor the author shall be liable for any physical, emotional, financial, psychological, or other damages incurred or allegedly incurred directly or indirectly from the information contained herein. Ultimately, the reader is responsible for his or her own choices, actions, and results.

The S.M.A.R.T. Sista's
Guide to College

*The secrets your parents, guidance counselors,
and campus advisors forgot to tell you!*

S.M.A.R.T.

Savvy   **M**ature   **A**dventurous   **R**esourceful   **T**asteful

SMART: stylish or elegant in dress or appearance, mentally alert, witty clever. Canny and shrewd in dealings with others, amusingly clever; witty

Part 1   Reputation

If there was only one thing I could share with you little Sistas it is, **protect your rep** (reputation). There is almost nothing worse than spending four years at a school being known as a campus 'ho/busdown/runner/... Yes I know some of those terms may be politically incorrect or offensive, but this is a book about the real world, not how we wish it would be. I promise to give it to you straight. So Sistas, even though we are in a new millennia, I assert that your reputation still matters and getting a bad one in college can be the difference between great memories and horrible nightmares. So I'm starting this book with the "secret" to living it up in college while not getting a bad rep!

The Keyword is "DISCRETION." Definition: 1. the quality of behaving so as to avoid social embarrassment or distress

This applies to your personal affairs. Really, who

wants to walk around campus knowing that everyone either knows, thinks they know, or is talking about the details of your intimate affairs? Now, if what you are going for is to have your name in everyone's mouth, please ignore this portion of the book. Skip ahead to the part about studying and making the grade because it is very possible to graduate with good grades and a bad reputation. Your choice.

Dating / Kicking It/ Hanging Out:

Dating on campus can be a joke or you can meet the love of your life. Some guys are there to get with as many women as possible and are not really interested in a relationship and to be fair; a lot of women are too. For the first time you are totally free to do what you want. If you are at a religious or historically black college, there may be *some* rules, but at most universities, there are no curfews, no dorm monitors, and heck the dorms may even be co–ed!

So what's a Sista to do? I could say "never, ever go into a boys room alone" or "do not date and just focus on your academics" but I said this was real talk so let's be real. You are going to date, kick it, or hang out with guys, so how do you do it safely AND without arousing suspicion and gossip? Read on Sista.

It is all about timing. Your first semester of college is crucial. It can set the tone for the rest of your experience and if you get off to a bad start, it will be hell trying to bounce back. Save yourself the trouble and follow these tips

- **Be out of his room/place by a reasonable hour**[1]

Let him walk you home and stay for a while but you need to be gone from his dorm/apt before it gets too late. First it will let him know that you have boundaries and that you are aware of and care about how you appear to the world. He may not like it, but if he is worth anything he will respect it.

Secondly, you will not be walking across campus alone late at night. College may seem like a dream world, but sometimes criminals stake out campuses just hoping to find naïve coeds wandering alone after dark. If he is any sort of a gentleman he will offer to walk you home, your safety should be your primary concern AND his. I'm not giving you a curfew or anything, but it is in your best interest to finish up on your turf!

- **Keep the Door Open:**

You think I'm being silly but it is the truth. You just got to college, you do not know him like that, even if you are old friends and have known each other since you were in diapers, nobody

---

[1] *I say reasonable hour because depending on where you go to school the actual time will vary. An easy guideline is that when the sunsets, you should be on your way home.*

else knows it so KEEP THE DOOR OPEN! It may sound old–fashioned but during the beginning of your friendship or first semester, if you decide to go hang out at his place, keep the door open, better yet, hang out in the common room/lobby.

The reasons are simple. For one, if the door is closed, people will speculate about what is going on, and since you have nothing to hide (because you just met this guy and I *know* you are not going to go "there" within the first couple of dates), this is the best policy to keep the tongue waggling to a minimum. Secondly knowing that anyone who walks by can see what you are up to will help you keep your wits about you. Trust me, I know it is hard to be sensible all the time (especially if you are really feeling him) so if you are going to be alone with him, perhaps keeping the public's eyes on you will help you keep it PG.

FYI! He will probably complain, but again it is about boundaries. Let him know upfront that while one day the door can be closed, you want to wait until you "get to know him better." Be straight with him about what your concerns are. He may not like it, but if he is worth your time he will respect your wishes and in turn respect you.

Respect is key and you set the tone from the start. Just think, if he complains too much at this simple precaution, I promise getting him to wear a condom or walk you home will be next to impossible and who wants to deal with that kind of drama later on! Let him know upfront that you take your safety and reputation seriously and you will save yourself a lot of trouble later.

• **Go Out in Public:**

Yes, the point of this book is to keep your business private, but that does not mean keep your relationship a secret. The reality is that once people know for sure you are a couple, they do not find the gossip that interesting. Go on dates; hold hands walking across the quad/yard/campus, etc... Yes, you are marking your territory, simultaneously letting other people know the two of you are involved, and establishing the precedent to take your relationship to the next level without dealing with the gossip.

The good thing is that nowadays people expect that you will be alone with your boyfriend so it is no big deal if you have the door closed or hang out late (maybe even over–night after much much much more time has passed). It is only juicy when there is the big question in the air about what's up with the two of you! So put the relationship out there for the world to see and eliminate the need to speculate!

Creeping is not cute!

There may be another name for it on your campus, but it boils down to the same thing. You are heading home early in the morning in the same clothes you had on last night hoping no one sees you because it is the crack of dawn.

FYI: there are people who just *live* to see who's doing the **"walk of shame."** These fools have nothing better to do than get up early in the morning and peep out their windows to check out who is coming from whose apartment/door–room or building. The walk of shame happens for a few reasons but it can easily be avoided if you use the information in this book.

If he cannot be seen with you on the quad/yard you cannot be seen leaving his place after hours. PERIOD

Look, if you are "seeing" a guy, there is no reason to keep your relationship a secret. Having people "all in your business" is different than having a "secret love affair." **FYI there is a reason he wants it to be a secret, HE IS SEEING 2, 3, 5, 10 OTHER GIRLS TOO!**

Sistas, when a man does not want the world to know he is with you then there are only a few reasons a couple of which are:

1. **He is embarrassed to be with you.** Need I say more? If he is embarrassed by you, he

is not worthy of your company

2. **He is not really available**: He has another girlfriend, heck maybe even a wife; now days he might have a boyfriend too!

3. **SOMETHING ELSE**: Who knows what, but to be safe my advice stands. If he is not willing to tell the world he is off the market, he is not.

Now if you are okay with being one of many or being kicked to the curb when a woman who respects herself comes along and captures his heart, please ignore this advice.

If your relationship is public and none of the above applies there is no reason you cannot leave a change of clothes and toiletries at his place to use in the AM right? So there is no big rush to get up, get home and get yourself together. You can take your time because you have all the essentials over there because you two are an item and do not care if the entire world knows!

If for some crazy reason you just do not want to have a boyfriend or do not care that he is seeing multiple people,[2] you must still **AVOID THE WALK OF SHAME AT ANY COST!**

Do not ever, ever, ever go to his place and stay the night. First, many boy's dorm rooms / apartments are more than a little dirty so why

---

[2] We need a have a little talk about safety, and judgment if you are here, but read on anyway

would you even want to go over there and stay? Have him come to your place and let him navigate those waters. I hate to say it, but there is still a double standard. If he is seen walking across campus in the wee hours of the morning everyone will be trying to figure out where he is coming from so they can talk about the girl he was with, but his reputation won't suffer at all. So my advice is to send him packing ASAP so everyone will not know your business. Again if you are in an established relationship with the fellow, let him keep or have some toiletries/ change of clothes there for him to use. That way it is no big deal (NBD). [3]

Make him walk you home: If you choose to ignore my advice and go to his place, then, have him walk you home. If he refuses, it is a sure fire red flag that he does not respect you. If that happens please be safe and do not walk across campus alone at night, call security or see if the school has an escort service. Then, kick this guy to the curb, he is an ass and **do not waste your time with him.**

If he wants to hang out in your room, in the common room, or outside your dorm for a little while longer fine, but always be safe and S.M.A.R.T!

---

[3] Make sure you run this by your roommate beforehand! Make sure she is okay with overnight male company or has time to make other arrangements.

Kicking It / Managing Multiple Men

So you are not looking for a relationship. You want to play the field and have a good time. Not a problem...unless you do not know how to manage your affairs. I am not suggesting you be a "playette", but hey if you want to sample the man buffet that is college, there is a S.M.A.R.T. way to handle it.

After you graduate and enter the real world, you can date as many people as you like and not have much to worry about in terms of people being in your business, but college is a lot different. It is a small little world and everyone is watching you. So how do you juggle 1, 2, 3 or more guys without getting a rep?

Strategy Tips: Keep your guys from very different communities! I had a friend who was a master of keeping her business on the down–low. If you ask anyone who went to school with us, she probably never even had a boyfriend. Now we (her girls) knew better but she handled her business so that it stayed private.

If you go to school in an area with a lot of colleges, pick guys from different schools. Make sure however they are not in the same Fraternity and/or play the same sports! If you are on an isolated campus, pick guys from different cliques! Maybe find someone local who may not be at your school. When I say different cliques I mean only 1 frat boy or 1 athlete or 1 artsy person. You have to minimize the chance that your suitors will talk to each other about you!

Let me be clear, I am not advocating cheating or lying, **however**; unless you and he specifically decide you are not seeing other people, you are free to do as you please. I do however want you to be S.M.A.R.T.

GETTING YOUR GROOVE ON

Do not have intimate relationships with multiple partners. It is high-risk behavior and not a S.M.A.R.T. move. A lot of people like to "experiment" in college. Do you really want to expose yourself to different diseases like that? If you are not in an exclusive relationship with a guy, assume he is dating other women and assume he is sleeping with them too. So while my advice is to wait until you are in a long–term committed relationship before being sexually active with anyone, if you choose to "get busy" always always always ALWAYS use a condom, only have 1 partner at a time, and get tested often.

FRESHMEAT!

How to handle the boys that would be beasts!

They are on every campus, laying in wait for the new class of freshman girls to hit the scene. Just like in high school, the upperclass*men* love to see a new crop of lovelies arrive on campus just ripe for the picking. What they do not know is that you are ready for them, and while you are going to have fun, you are a S.M.A.R.T. Sista and will not be played.

Not every boy that shows interest in you should get your goodies!

So, one of the first things that happens when you get to a campus is you notice the cute boys that are every-where!! They are checking you out and you are doing the same. "Hey, what's your name? Where are you from? What dorm are you in living in?" Okay, the game comes fairly easy for some and a little harder for others. But there are some things that you should know first. Do not give your goodies to every little knucklehead that shows you some attention. If you do, you could possibly end up a) sleeping with too many boys; b) you get a dis-ease c) you get a jacked up reputation or d) all of the above or a few combinations. So, here are some things that you should consider.

1) While college is definitely a place where most people will lose their virginity (that is just the truth of the matter) if you decide to do so, be very selective with whom you sleep with. Set your standards high and do not lower them. Everyone that you meet does not de-serve to have you. Keep your numbers low. Think about it, by the time you finally decide on one man to marry, do you really want to think about giving yourself to him knowing that you slept with 50 other people!! Gross!! **So, keep the numbers low.**

2) Upper class men love to prey on the fresh meat. Why? For the most part, you are new to freedom and they know it. They think that freshmen are easy con-quests. Most girls are just happy to be out of their parent's house. They are free and their legs are easily opened. Do not fall for the okeydoke!! No matter how fine he may be, get to know the brother first. I do not say that they are off limits totally, just really get to know them and then decide. I do not recommend going to their dorm rooms or off campus apartments however.

3) Date rape is real and you do not want to put your-self in a compromising position without any options. If you decide to go to a guy's crib, make sure that you tell someone where you are going and give them a phone number. If something goes down, you will want to be found by someone. But if at all possible, have your friend come to your dorm. That way, you are in your comfort zone and hopefully you have friends that you have given signals to so they know if they should inter-rupt if you feel uncomfortable with your guest.

4) Get to know people before giving up the goods. Most folks show you their true colors after a few encounters. If they are crazy, an idiot, a player, etc, it will most likely be revealed within a few visits. So, get to know people. Do not be surprised if you sleep with someone after saying hey and then they act crazy. Well, you just played yourself because you did not know him. You would have if you just waited a while. Some people will be worthy of the goods and some will not, so be selec-tive!!

I couldn't have said it better myself. The contribu-tor of that tip is one of those Divas who had a lot of fun in college and always kept it discreet. While she liked the boys she was not willing to let herself be used and abused by anyone!

Next are a few stories about how some of my friends and I dealt with some the typical campus predators.

THE ATHLETE

Kevin was a tall handsome basketball player on cam-pus. We had been talking on the phone for a while and he asked me if I wanted to "go for a walk" (that is code for go somewhere private to talk for a little and then a make–out session). Everyone was really excited because he was an athlete and it was a coup for me to be "cho-

*sen"! So we go for a walk and find ourselves at the
bleachers. As soon as we get there, he just "attacks me"
I was like "Whoa, slow down, let's get to know each
other a little better." As soon as I put the breaks on, he
stood up and left me sitting there!*

*I went to school in the country so it was dark and I was
all the way across campus and he did not care that I
would have to walk home alone. It was well known
that many women had been attacked walking alone at
night. He was a jerk like many (not all) star athletes/
high profile men who sometimes feel so entitled that
when you say no they get indignant. Luckily he did not
lie and say we did anything, but even so, I was scared
walking back to my dorm and am thankful that nothing happened to me. From that point on he would not
even look my way or acknowledge my existence. Just
think how much worse I would have felt if I actually
had slept with him!*

It is fine to date athletes or other campus stars just
make sure you do not get caught up in the hype and
pressure of a high–profile relationship and agree to
do things that you are not okay with. Do a check–
in with yourself about your comfort level with the
speed at which your relationship progresses. Often
these guys are on a quest to "get" as many of the
new girls on campus as possible so take your time
and see what his intentions truly are. In the story
above, the odds are that even if she did let things
go further he would not have kept seeing her anyway. His actions made it clear what he was after,
better she learn it before she shared her body with
him.

THE GORGEOUS GUY

> *He was one of the most handsome guys on campus. I felt so lucky that he wanted to be with me. We were "talking" for 2 months. I thought we really had a connection. He drove me to the airport, carried my bags and was really sweet. We talked all over Christmas break and I was looking forward to seeing him when I got back to campus. He wanted to have sex and I was not ready, the next thing I knew, he just stopped calling. I never heard from him again. He was not mean; he just ignored me. I felt so bad that I had sex with the very next guy I dated even though I was not ready emotionally. I regret it to this day*

Unfortunately some men are only out for one thing and if you do not have sex with them they will move on to the next girl/woman who will. Yes it will hurt, especially if you really like him, but do want to think back in 5, 10, 15, 20 years and regret being pressured into something you did not want to do?

The woman above felt so bad and was so scared about another guy dropping her that she pushed herself to do something that she was not ready for and regrets it. **There is nothing wrong with being single and/or waiting for sex until *YOU* are comfortable.** If a guy is unwilling to respect your wishes or wait, HE IS NOT THE GUY FOR YOU! Dating and being in relationships should be fun not pressure–filled. I for one had many male friends who loved me for me and I am sure that they were sleeping with other women, but I am the one they took out to dinner and treated like a queen! I will be honest I did not "date"[4] a whole lot of men in college. However, I did spend a lot of quality time with awesome men. Often men look at college as a time to sleep with as many women as possible and unless you are willing to play that game and be used, you may spend some time alone. The thing is being alone/single does not mean being lonely! I had lots of male and female friends and I was never lonely.

THE "OFF-CAMPUS" DATE

He and I had been talking for a couple of weeks. Lots of time spent talking on the phone "getting to know" each other. One Saturday after spending all afternoon talking he invited me out to dinner. I agreed and was excited. When he suggested we go back to his place to watch movies I said yes and was very clear with him that I did not want to have sex. He was like "Okay, I just want to make you feel good." He wanted to just "use his hands" True to form, I was enjoying the experience, but the next thing I know, I feel both his hands caressing my body, yet I was still feeling a sensation down below! I quickly came to my senses and was like "NO! I am not ready to have sex!" Luckily, he was a nice guy and respected my wishes, but things really could have been different. I was off-campus in the country with no way home! If I had been on campus it would have been much easier for me to escape if things got out of hand.

I do not recommend going "back to his place" if he lives off-campus. You do not know the lay of the land and if you get caught out there with a crazy, how are you going to get home? Just because they

---

[4] By "date" I mean sleep with, be romantic with, and/or be in a relationship with.

have an apartment and not a dorm room, the same rules apply. Do not go to his off–campus apartment if you have no way to get home, until you know him...well. A couple of weeks are not enough time to get to know someone. Refer back to my earlier notes to invite him to your place, just arrange for some alone time with your roommate in advance!

THE INTELLECTUAL, FRATERNITY BOY, ARTIST, ETC...

I had several guy friends who were "nice." They were so sweet and kind that I just loved them to death and wanted to date them. I had a super crush on one of my really good friends and finally told him about it our senior year. He told me that he loved me and that he couldn't date me. I asked him why and he said that I was the kind of girl he would marry, not date while in college.

I was confused because as far as I knew he wasn't dating anyone. He and I always went out together and spent a lot of time together on campus. In fact he was my emergency date if I had a semi–formal to go to and didn't have an official date. It was almost like he was my boyfriend, but there was no physicality. My feelings were hurt because I thought he was just letting me down easy and really didn't find me attractive.

After talking to a few of my friends it turns out he had dated a number of women in my sorority and many many other women on the down low! His nice–guy persona had all the women thinking he was just low–key/private and not a player at all!

I asked him about it years later and he confessed that for him college was about getting a degree and that because he knew I was a quality woman he would not disrespect me by having a fling and treat me like that.

That is a personal story and the point is the women

who dated him were hurt because he would not go public with their "relationship." If you follow my advice you will not find yourself in that situation. On the other hand you may be single for minute, but being single does not mean you cannot have a lot of fun!

No matter what their label or campus status they are all men and should be treated the same. Players come in many forms, do not think because he *seems* nice when you first meet that he is, be S.M.A.R.T. and get to know him. Do not let anyone fill your head with empty promises and smooth talk. At the same time do not judge a guy just because he may be high profile, there ARE nice guys out there and part of being S.M.A.R.T. is being able to distinguish the difference.

I made up in my mind that I would not date any high–profile guys because they were all" players." I did not want to be a statistic and always worried about what he was doing when he was off–campus. I knew how girls like to throw themselves at the superstars so I would not consider athletes or campus stars. When I look back at my collegiate experience I can see several nice guys that I let slip past because I lumped them all in the same category. I guess my advice would be to evaluate each guy based on his actions not his activities or affiliations. Stereotyping and judging is never a good idea.

Final Thoughts

My friends and I want to be clear, you are in college to enjoy yourself and experience life. That life includes boys/men, but we also want you to be S.M.A.R.T. If you follow our advice and watch for the signs, you will be able to figure out pretty easily what a guy is all about. The most important thing is to **respect yourself and to demand that he respects you too.** Once you set that tone everything should be fine. If you are looking to have fun and keep it light, its ok, but you still want to be safe and protect yourself physically and emotionally. Be straight with yourself about who you are hanging out with. If he is a player be sure not to get your heart broken. The last thing you want to happen is to be distracted from your studies because you are recovering from a bad break–up. The main reason you are in school is to get an education, never forget that!

Part 2   Making the Grade

So I covered the topic of boys, let's move on to the reason you went to college in the first place, getting your education. College is a lot different than high school. If you are going to stay on top of your classes and do well, you have to work S.M.A.R.T. not hard. Following are some of the best strategies I picked up over the years for enjoying school and getting the best grades possible.

What do I want to be when I grow up?

PICKING A MAJOR

One of the most stressed over decisions in college is "What should I major in?" In reality, it is unrealistic to think you will enter college knowing exactly what you want to do for the rest of your life. If you already have a major it may be based on what your parents think you should do or what you think will make you the most money. Here is the deal, there is almost no amount of money to compensate for a job you hate. Listen to a Sista who has been out in the working world, it really pays to find a passion and turn it into a profession. With that said even if you are really really really confident that you have it down I still have some suggestions.

VISIT THE CAREER COUNSELING CENTER

This is a great resource most people do not discover until close to graduation when they are trying to find a job. Find the one on your campus ASAP and get a counselor! One of the first things they should have you take is an **interest inventory/personality/skills test**. Be honest with the answers. Do not skew the results to give the answer you think you want to hear. These tests can give you great insight into your personality; skill set, and correlated careers. As you have more experiences you may find that your interests will shift, so pay at least one visit a year to see if anything new has developed.

ELECTIVES ARE FANTASTIC

Even if you have a double major like bio–medical and electrical engineering, take a couple of fun classes. You can always make up a class or two in summer school. If you have a secret passion or something you enjoy, take a class or at least join a club/organization related to it.

I took some great classes like yoga, ceramics, weight training, and dance. I found that I really enjoyed them. Now almost 15 years later, I still do yoga and have no fear about going into the gym and using the equipment because I learned the proper way to use the machines in college. As for ceramics, I have not gotten back behind a pottery wheel since then, but I have taken other art classes for fun as a result of how much I enjoyed that experience! I would say that my electives helped me figure out some things that ended up being hobbies; things that I enjoy doing for fun. In dance I found a career path that I never would have expected so thank God for electives.

Study Strategies
SYLLABUS? WHAT IS THAT!

This is a special treat that you normally do not get in high school! Your professor will outline everything you are going to cover and when! The best way to make use of your syllabus is to **get a monthly planner and fill in all the test dates and paper/project due dates**. That way you will know when you have a heavy workload coming up and can plan in advance.

PLAN YOUR WORK & WORK YOUR PLAN

Take some time at the beginning of the semester to plan backwards. By that I mean look at the due date for a paper and/or the details for the assignment. If it is a long paper look back in your calendar and pick: a day to get started, a day to be half finished, and a day to have the first draft completed. Same thing for tests, pick a day and time to study for all your upcoming tests and write them in your calendar. That is how you **PLAN YOUR WORK**. Then make sure you actually do what you put on your schedule, that is **WORKING YOUR PLAN.** If you use this strategy, you will find that it is rare that you are surprised or overwhelmed with too much work to do because you planned it all out in advance!

BE PREPARED
READ BEFORE CLASS!

I used to wonder how some students were always able to ask such great questions in class. First I thought they were super smart and just automatically understood everything the professor said. Then one day I found out that they read the syllabus and went over the material before they got to class. That way they could ask the professor questions in class about anything they did not understand. With this tip I spent less time studying and school became even easier!

You will not believe how much more you will understand if you are not getting the information for the first time when you professor presents it! **Take the time to read the chapter before you get to class.** You will be able to ask questions and you will look really good to your professor for being prepared in advance!

You may ask, "how can I read in advance if I do not have the syllabus until the first day of class?" Often the syllabus is available online. You can go to the bookstore to see the books needed for your classes and buy them ahead of time. You can also visit the professor and get an advance copy of the syllabus. This is also a great time to introduce yourself to the professor and make sure he/she knows your name/face!

STUDY GROUPS: YOUR SECRET WEAPON

Do not spend all your time studying. Find a group of people to work with and work as a team. This is not cheating, its collaborative learning. In the real world you will have to learn to work with people to get the job done.

> *I majored in Electrical Engineering and spent almost every Friday night of my first semester in the computer lab finishing up homework. I missed out on sooo much fun because I thought that working on a team to solve the problem would be cheating. I even had a friend try to help me out and I refused. Later on I finally figured it out and got it confirmed by a professor. I felt so silly and still look back and think about all the good times I missed on Friday afternoon because I was determined to figure it all out by myself.*

HOW TO PICK GROUP MEMBERS

Do not mix business with pleasure. It is best you learn this lesson now, not in the workplace. Do not **pick your friends to be your study group members. Pick the best students, period.** If your friends fit the bill so be it, but you are in school to get the best grades and need to make it your business to study with students with the same intention.

Share the Load

When you get problem set, divide the questions up between everyone. Then make enough copies so you can share. Each group member should be able to explain how they came to answer and everyone should check to make sure it is correct. If you do not understand everything its okay, just make a note of it and go to your professor for extra help. You do not have to understand 100% of the homework to get 100% credit!

It is Okay Not To Know

ASK FOR HELP! You are not supposed to know everything, so do not try to "look good" and not tell anyone when you are struggling with something.

Most campuses actually have FREE TUTORS! Can you believe it? There are people available to help you with difficult classes for FREE! If you do not go and take advantage of this service you are not being S.M.A.R.T! The people in college want you to succeed so they put all these resources in place for you to use to make the best grades. S.M.A.R.T. Sistas know what to look for!

TEST BANKS: THE BEST KEPT SECRET EVER!

Did you know that many student organizations keep files of old tests organized by subject and professor? They are called test banks and they are a secret weapon to acing exams and quizzes!

WHERE TO FIND THEM

Check in student associations such as NSBE (National Society of Black Engineers) or The BSA (Black Student Alliance) sororities, fraternities, or maybe even the department! Yes many schools actually have archives of old tests on file for you to

review! Test Banks are not illegal, but not everyone knows they exist or why they are so valuable.
Isn't it nice to be a S.M.A.R.T. Sista![5]

HOW TO USE THEM

Many professors have a signature style when it
comes to their quizzes, tests and exams. Sometimes they actually just recycle questions from past
tests or use the exact same test every couple of
years! By practicing how to answer questions they
have asked in the past you can get clear on what
they are looking for or what types of questions they
may ask. If you are really lucky, they will use the
exact same questions and it will be that much
easier for you to answer them since you have seen
them before. **Please note:** Old tests and quizzes
should not be the only thing you use to study, but
using them in conjunction with reviewing your
notes and homework assignments will give you the
S.M.A.R.T. edge when exam time rolls around!

---

[5] At the end of the semester, make sure you donate your old tests & quizzes.
Black out your name if you like, but always give back!

My Friend the Professor
OFFICE HOURS: WHAT ARE THEY FOR?

Believe it or not your teacher will give you the answer! Whether you are writing a paper or completing a problem set, take your assignment to your professor and ask them to check it for you! They will tell you what is wrong and help you understand how to fix it. They will read your paper, edit it, and give it back so you can make corrections. Really there is almost no reason you cannot get 100% on all your assignments. All you have to do is not wait until the last minute and get really cool with your professor! So when you put all your due dates in your monthly student planner, take a moment to decide when you will start your assignments and plan for enough time to have your professor look it over before it is due so you have time to make the corrections he/she will recommend.

On a side note, if you are on the border between an A and A+ or a C+ or B– the relationship you have with your professor can be the difference between the higher and lower grade.

Make friends with your profession, however; if he or she tries ANYTHING funny, tell the dean!

Part 3 Making Memories

Campus Life

FRIENDS AND FOES

YOUR CREW

Everyone needs a crew to run the campus with. It may be 1 or 2 girls, or you may end up with a posse of 10, but you have to find someone to confide in and hang with.

HOW TO MEET THEM

If you do not make friends easily, the best advice I can give you is to join some clubs that interest you! The best thing about college is that there is a club or organization for anything you can imagine: drama, hiking, writing, photography, bug collecting, politics, the list is endless! There you will find people that you have at least 1 thing in common with. It is a great place to start when looking for friends.

At the beginning of the academic year almost every campus has a club and student organization fair. All the different groups set up tables in the student center or somewhere on main campus and you can sign up for the ones that interest you. MAKE SURE YOU DO NOT MISS THIS EVENT. This is the easiest way to see all the fun things campus has to offer and connect with other students who have similar interests. Hands down this is the BEST way to start making friends. Go to the meetings, volunteer for committees and stay involved. We'll talk more about this later!

ROOMMATES

You often have no say over whom you are going to live with in college. If you are lucky like me you'll get her contact information before you arrive so you can talk, email, connect online and coordinate who is bringing what to the room. On the other hand, you may have no idea what she'll be like and have to be prepared for ANYTHING.

If you have different neatness styles now is the time to learn about acceptance & consideration. I happen to be a little messy and my roommate was a neat freak. I made an effort to keep my mess contained to my side of the room and she learned to accept everything not being perfect! I will be honest there was some tension and to this day my apartment has piles of paper here and there, but in being considerate I made it a point to straighten up my area every couple of days. It is no fun to live in a tense environment.

On the other hand later I had a roommate that liked to entertain men...a lot and it made me a little uncomfortable. Rather than get upset and mad I sat down and talked with her about it and we set some ground rules. She agreed to not have company every night and to let me know in advance if she needed some privacy. Luckily we worked it out, but it does not always work out that way.

My freshman roommate always had men in the dorm room. It was crazy because sometimes they would stay overnight! I was not comfortable with having her boyfriend staying every night. I felt like I could never relax in my own room. I would talk to her about it and she would promise to cut back, but after a couple of weeks it would be exactly the same. I started not being in my room at all because it was so stressful and I was really angry. It got to the point where we stopped speaking, but her behavior didn't change until they broke up.

Thinking back, I should have gone to the RA (Resident Advisor) and had her handle it instead of just "taking it." My advice would be that if you find yourself in a roommate situation where you are not comfortable and your roommate is not willing to work it out with you, go to the RA and have them settle it!

Living with a stranger can be a challenge, and even if you shared a room at home with your sister this is different. First you want to try to work out any issues with your roommate directly. When you have this conversation make sure you do not accuse her of being bad or wrong. Just share how whatever is going on makes you feel and request her partnership in finding a solution. For example:

"Roommate, I really like to live in a neat and orderly environment. The room/apartment is kind of messy and it is hard for me to focus or be relaxed when it's like this. Are you willing to work with me to create a system to keep the room/apartment clean?"

vs.

"Roommate, you are really messy and I'm tired of cleaning up after you. You need to do a better job of cleaning up after yourself, I'm not your maid."

Always avoid using the word YOU and/or focusing on her or her behavior. If this approach does not work or she gets upset or is unwilling to work with you, take it to the next level. Go see your RA (Resident Advisor).[6]

Whatever you do, if you are unhappy with your roommate situation, do not just "take it." First see if you can open your mind and be a little more accepting and/or considerate. If the situation is having an impact on your well–being get into action to resolve it. This is an opportunity for you to grow up and start fighting your own battles. Do not automatically run to your parents, but do some-

---

[6] *Most dorms have an upperclassman that stays on your floor and/or hall that is there to mediate roommate disputes and assist you with adjusting to campus life.*

thing. If talking to your roommate and the RA does not get the situation handled, by all means let your parents know what is going on so they can assist you. There are resources available to you and you should never be nervous or afraid to go home and be in your room/apartment.

TO BE OR NOT TO BE GREEK: SORORITY LIFE

I know that the sorority thing is not for everyone, and I am happy that I joined a sorority while in college. If you are considering pledging there are some key things to consider.

Do I want to be in a sorority?

Which one should I choose?

Pan–Hellenic Council Sororities vs. Historically Black Sororities

There are very different intake processes for these groups. While no sorority is permitted to discriminate based on race or ethnicity, it should be noted that historically black sororities (Delta Sigma Theta, Alpha Kappa Alpha, Sigma Gamma Rho. Zeta Phi Beta) have their roots in the African American Culture.

RUSHING & PLEDGING

No matter what sorority path you walk, the first step is figuring out which is best for you. Every group has its own style and the best advice I can give is to not only find out about the official history of each group, but to consider how they operate on your campus!

While your entire family may have pledged a particular organization, the chapter on your campus may or may not work for you. If that is the case you may have to consider breaking tradition and joining another group, staying independent, or joining at the graduate level (if that is an option).

What I can tell you is that you will not have great memories of fun and sisterhood if you are trying to be part of a group that you do not click with. Do not try to force it. If the Delta's on your campus are known for partying hard and you are more of a homebody, you will be frustrated trying to relate.

Once you decide if and which group is for you, the next step is Rush. Here is where the two types of sororities tend to differ. At many schools the Historically Black Sororities hold their Rush independent of the Pan Hellenic Sororities.

If you have followed my advice and started participating in campus activities and are selecting a sorority based on common interests you should know at least one member in your Sorority of choice. I recommend asking some questions discreetly, but PLEASE make sure you have done some independent research BEFORE approaching her. If you do not know any members personally make sure you attend ALL their events and activities so that they know your face and start to get to know them! No one wants to think you only want to be their friend so you can get in their sorority. No one likes to be used. If you cannot genuinely find a reason to befriend anyone in your organization of choice, perhaps you want to rethink your choice.

So you think you wanna be a ....

You have been waiting to get to college so that you can join a sorority and step!! You can hardly wait. Well, there are some general things that you should know. Now, if you already know what you want to join because your mom is a Delta or all of your family is AKA, that is great. But, if you want to join one but you do not know which one is right for you, you need to do two things:

1. Do your own research about the available sororities on your campus. Go on line, look at their history, their mission statement and try to find the one that is most like what you believe is most aligned with your personal beliefs. The internet or library books can give you a good idea. Do not go by who steps the best at the step show because that is just superficial.

2. Look at the chapter of women on your campus. Do you like what you saw? Are they doing things that are respectable? Do they seem to be women with great character and morals? If you like what you see and you like the history of the organization, I say you have found the one for you, if you like one but not the other (for example if you like the history but not the women) you make the call.

Once you have made up YOUR MIND as to which one you would like to join, here are some general rules. Make sure you know what you want and do not waiver, people see that as confused and you do not want anyone to think of you as being confused!

1. Attend events, service projects, seminars, work-shops, or whatever that sorority is doing on your campus or in the community. Now, this is important for two reasons. It is important to know what things they are doing so that you will have an idea of what you will be doing when you are in. Moreover, it is important for the members of the sorority to get to know you. They will see your face and get to know your name, which is good. If you want to be a part of an organization, isn't it a good idea to see what they do? So, go!! Be respectful, speak, and be yourself.

2. Start doing your research to find out about the his-tory of the sorority. It is good to know some information that will make your time on line less stressful. If the sorority was founded on community service, you may what to do some community service and have a history of doing service before joining the sorority.

3. Try to get to know at least one member of the soror-ity really well. You may have a class with them or they live in your dorm. Befriend them. Be nice and get to be comfortable with them. When you are ready, express your interest in the sorority to them. They will tell you what to do next.

4. Last but not least, keep your grades up. Study and make sure that you are on point with your grades. Every sorority requires a minimum GPA so know what that is but keeps your grades even higher than that ex-pectation. That way, if your grades slip a little on line, you still have the grades to be okay. If you make the minimum and they slip on line, you may be hit!

HAZING

When I was president of my chapter we were suspended for hazing. In all honestly according the official definition, we did haze those girls, and I want to be clear we did not engage in ANY activi-ties that would have threatened their health or well–being. That being said the rules clearly stated that we were not to have an interest group, meet with them, or require them to do anything as a condition of joining the organization and we did so we were suspended.

Regardless, I promised you real talk and if you plan to join a sorority I recommend you connect with other women who are interested, make it your business to be at all Sorority sponsored events and activities, and get to know as many chapter members as possible. At the same time, do not compromise yourself.

The whole sorority thing can be nerve–wracking, but here are some tips to keep in mind when rushing/pledging:

- **DO NOT LET ANYONE Disrespect you**
  I do not care how much you want to be in a sorority, do not let anyone treat you inhumanely. There is a difference between being humble, showing respect, and being disrespected.

  Yes we did some silly things like running errands, cooking dinners, and being of service to our Big Sisters, but we were never mistreated in any shape form or fashion.

- **Know Your Limits**: Do not participate in any activity that would be in conflict with your well–being or personal beliefs.

  One of my Sorority sisters is Muslim and another was a 7th Day Adventist, our Big Sisters never asked them to compromise their religious beliefs or customs to pledge. Yes we were very tired trying to balance school and the pledging process, but our health and safety were never at–risk. If you are pledging and feel like your health or safety is at risk tell

*someone (the advisor and/or the dean over soror-
ity/fraternity life).*

- **Be A United Front**: You and your line sisters should
  support one another and if one person is a
  "No"(meaning she does not want to do something) to a
  request you all should be a "No." Do not pressure anyone into doing something she is not comfortable with.

- **There is a difference between HARD and DAN-
  GEROUS**: Just because something takes some effort
  does not mean it is dangerous. Anything worth having you should be willing to work for. In reality once
  you get into the sorority it will be a HUGE demand on
  your time and energy.

  Part of the pledging process is seeing how well you
  can balance the added demands of sorority life. If you
  want it, be willing to work hard and make some sacri-
  fices.

- **If you do not trust the chapter members STOP**:
  If you think the women in the chapter are going to
  abuse or mistreat you, do not join or stop the action
  and alert someone in authority.

Always be S.M.A.R.T. and you can get through
anything, including pledging!

SPRING BREAK

If there is one thing I regret, it is not having more fun on Spring Break! In the real world, there are no scheduled spring breaks. No time of the year when you can be guaranteed to have thousands of your peers from all across the country in one place ready to do nothing but PARTY!! So my advice is to go every year and have a great time, the S.M.A.R.T. WAY. At the beginning of the year there will be people and posters on campus advertising spring break packages. Get your friends together and pick a package. **Before you put any money down be sure to research the travel company and make sure they are reputable.** Remember S.M.A.R.T. Sistas are resourceful and will not be one of the suckers waiting at the airport for the charter plane that never arrives! Most of these companies know that college students do not have big money so not only are the trips priced affordably, many have payment plans that will allow you to pay on your trip throughout the fall and first half of the spring!

SPRING BREAK ON A BUDGET

If your money is really tight or you like to be really resourceful consider becoming a trip organizer/recruiter! All you have to do is convince other students to go on a trip with your company and your trip will be free! I recommend finding a company during the summer before the school year starts. Again do your research before signing up; you do not want to be the person who represented the rip–off artists.

BIG FUN W/O REGRETS!

So now that you are on Spring Break do not ruin it by forgetting to be S.M.A.R.T. Having fun does not equal losing your mind. I do not want to hear about any S.M.A.R.T. Sistas on one of "those" videos!

Nowadays almost everyone has camera and/or videophones so you never know who is watching. It is possible to have fun without doing anything that will come back to haunt you on campus or in your post–collegiate life.

HOOKING UP

Flirting is good, random "hook ups" not so good. Safety is always number one so having "relations" with perfect strangers is not a good idea. So how far do you go? Well this is one of those gray areas, but I will try to offer a little guidance.

Campus Connection: Find a cutie from campus and set the stage for a hook–up before spring break. Flirt a little, ask him where he is going for break and suggest that you would like to hang out together down there. If there is someone you have your eye on, this may be the perfect opportunity to make your move!

The Fling: Rather than look back at a blur of hook–ups have a fling. Find a guy and spend a lot of time with him during your break. These mini–relationships rarely last after the final goodbye, but they make for great memories so take lots of pictures!

PARTYING

Believe it or not, you do not have to spend your Spring Break drunk! I am not saying drinking is bad, BUT being incoherent and unable to make good decisions is not S.M.A.R.T. or safe. If you have to be wasted in order to have a good time I suggest you seek professional help to figure out why it is so hard for you to loosen up.

The thing about drinking is that it should be done responsibly. Even some old people do not get this concept. Being drunk is not a valid excuse for making poor decisions. So how do you navigate these waters?

Designate a lookout: Switch off nights for someone to look out for the group each night. This S.M.A.R.T. Sista will try to keep tabs on everyone and make sure nothing is getting out of hand. Just because you have a lookout, you do not have the go ahead to get drunk and out of control. **No one is responsible for you**, but the lookout should be on alert for anything that could be really dangerous. So if you are in a corner kissing on some random loser, she is not going to pull you apart, but if she sees you about to walk out the door with him, she would stage an intervention. If you decide to get on the bar and dance around the pole or in the cage, it is up to you, but if you start taking off your clothes, it is time to call it a night!

Stay with the group: Make a pact to stay together no matter what. Even if you meet a super cute guy, get his number and arrange catch up with him the next day when you are sober, if he is that hott, and really interested he will be open to it. When you are intoxicated your decision–making is impaired. You may not be able to make a good assessment of his character in an altered state. Your best bet is to arrive with your crew and leave with your crew. Now if you all decide to go as a group fine because your lookout will still be around and able to keep an eye on things.

Do not go home alone with strangers: If you meet someone who is irresistible, invite him back to your place for some quality time. The same rules apply on break or on campus. No wandering the streets alone late at night. Have him come over and hang out in the room, by the pool, in the lobby, or on the beach. It is not a S.M.A.R.T. move to be alone at some guys hotel/villa/condo in a strange place without your crew to back you up or able to come to your aid if things start to go south. If you just have to go to his spot, take at least one person from your crew. If no one is up to it, get his number and arrange to meet him the next day in a public place.

EXPAND YOUR HORIZONS:

Study Abroad / Campus Exchange

One of the only things I really regret was not taking advantage of our Study Abroad or Campus Exchange programs. After taking 4 years of Spanish in high school and continuing in college, I wanted to immerse myself in the language for a few months and become fluent. Instead I let my fear of going to a strange country stop me. Now I look back and could just kick myself! Don't be like me, be S.M.A.R.T.

Almost EVERY University has some sort of formal relationship with a sister school somewhere in the country and/or world. I cannot emphasize enough the wonderful opportunity this presents you with Sistas. Studying abroad or at another school is an opportunity to experience a different culture and expand your network even further! Whether you go overseas or just to another school across the country, find out about the program(s) available on your campus.

If for some reason your school does not have a formal program in place look online and search for "Study Abroad" or "Campus Exchange" programs. You could spend a semester, summer, or entire year on an exciting adventure. There are scholarships available and often your tuition will transfer over too. As for your grades, your credits should transfer as well and if not, take some electives Pass/Fail, but make sure you DO IT!

DRUGS & ALCOHOL

Yes I am going to take it here. In reality there are drugs and alcohol on college campuses and many people will partake. I would LOOOOVE to say, "Just say no," but I said I would keep it real so here it goes.

BE RESPONSIBLE. That is open ended because even a few of our president's admit to trying a few things in their youth. So here are some real life tips about these controversial topics

- IF YOU ARE GOING TO TRY DRUGS do not try ANYTHING in an unfamiliar environment: Be around friends that you TRUST!!! Do not be around anyone (men or women) who you do not know well.

- NEVER leave your drink unattended! There are all kinds of drugs that can and may be slipped in without you noticing it.

- HAVE A BUDDY! Rotate nights and have a designated S.M.A.R.T. Sista who is on the lookout for everyone else to make sure you get home safely and do not get caught in a dangerous situation (i.e.: drunk or high in someone's room doing something you may regret and/or may not remember in the morning). This S.M.A.R.T. Sista will periodically check on everyone at the party.

- Learn the art of deception. Have 1 DRINK and sip it all night! Lemon/lime soda with a lime, coke with a lime. I get wanting to "fit in" but who knows what is really in your glass?

- DO NOT GET DRUNK: You do not have to be out of control to have fun. Learn to enjoy alcohol responsibly. Being buzzed is different than being drunk.[7] 1 drink per hour on a full stomach tends to be a good rule of thumb. Being BUZZED is just like being a little "happy" the inhibitions are loosened but not totally gone.

▪ AVOID DRUGS: Nowadays you do not know what anything is laced with. You may think you are trying marijuana and it may really be laced with PCP or who knows what. I know it sounds old–fashioned, but do you really want to wake–up naked somewhere wondering what went down? With the camera phones and other technology do you want to risk photos and/or video of you hitting the net and following you for the next 4 years or longer. I get that you want to fit in, but you and the other S.M.A.R.T. Sistas must stand together and decide IT IS NOT WORTH IT. PERIOD!

My advice, leave the drugs alone and enjoy alcohol responsibly.

COMMUNITY

Enough with the heavy stuff, let's get back to the fun! One of the keys to having a great college experience is building a strong community and being involved. Now my very best friend is a community service junkie where I was more into clubs and community organizations. The thing is, in our own way we both gave back. I wrote for the paper and served in Student Government and she tutored in the community. We both joined a sorority and had tons of fun! I highly recommend mixing it up with a combination of service and

---

[7] Although you should not drive in either state.

personal interest activities.

CLUBS & STUDENT ORGANIZATIONS

Earlier I mentioned getting involved in clubs and student organizations as a great way to meet friends and get connected. This is the perfect way to expand yourself, get to know yourself, and have a full rich life. When you first get to campus and attend the Club & Organization Fair, go crazy. Sign up to get information about ANY & EVERYTHING that interests you. Go to at least one meeting and check out the vibe and the people. You may start to see some people at multiple events and see an opportunity to start a friendship.

The key is to find a group of people, a project or activity that you care about or are interested in (politics, dance, children, adolescents, elderly, environment, skiing, music, etc) and find a group or organization related to it. I encourage you to try something new AND continue with things you already enjoy. If you danced in high school, try out for the dance team or another group. If you always wanted to be in a play, check out a theatre group. College is the BEST place to experience things you always wondered about, but never had the opportunity to try. I remember we had a Sky Diving Club! I never actually did it because I was scared and now I wish I had, so do not hold back.

COMMUNITY SERVICE

As a part of the human race, I think we all are here to give back and make a difference, so find at least one way to be of service to your community while on campus.

Here is what my best friend had to say on the subject.

Why would you want to spend time helping a group of people that you do not know and are not getting paid to help? Good question. It builds character, it helps you to think of someone else other than yourself and you should help someone else. It is your responsibility to give back to the community, so start now.

There are probably some service groups that are already established and do some good work. If not, you can always find some causes that you feel passionate about and you can organize a community service project.

For example, there may be a group that tutors little children at a community center, or a group that goes to a nursing home to help take care of the elderly. If your school has a hospital associated with it, you can volunteer at the hospital as a candy striper or you can work in a particular unit like the cardiac unit or the pediatric ward.

In any case, it is important that you become a part of the community in which you are living for the next few years. Not only does it make you feel valuable, you are doing a good deed for others.

THE FRESHMAN 15

If you haven't heard the term, one of the things that typically happens when people go off to college is weight gain. We call it the "Freshman 15." You can thank me later, because I am going to share the secret to avoid packing on the pounds during your freshman year.

If you were an athlete in high school and are not playing a sport in college you have to maintain a similar level of diet and exercise as you did at home and/or be conscious of your lifestyle and eating habits. On campus you will have access to all sorts of junk food and alcohol, the biggest culprits for empty calories. Those late–night study sessions can easily turn into pizza parties that turn into the dreaded Freshman 15.

You will stay up late studying, or want to go out to eat after partying, and while you may get hungry at night, do not call and order a pizza or a sub every day or every other day. Have some control and be S.M.A.R.T.! Late night eating and junk food = weight gain! In fact the weight gain, may happen faster because you usually did not eat so late, and/or eat junk food all the time when you lived at home.

The great news is that you can make it through and maintain your fabulousness. Follow these tips.

- Monitor your food especially after 8 pm at night. If you do eat late pick something light or only have 1 slice of pizza not 3 or 4.
- If you are studying late at night make sure you BRING SNACKS WITH YOU. Go to the grocery store and stock up on some fresh fruit or good nutritious snacks like chips & salsa, nuts, dried fruit, and trail mix.
- Make good choices about what you eat on a day–to–day basis. Balanced meals with salads, grilled or steamed veggies, lean protein, fruits and grains are very beneficial. **Do not base your entire diet on fries, pizza, desserts, fatty foods and bread**. I know you are going to eat junk food, but eat it in moderation.
- **WORK OUT:** The work out facility at the college campus is usually really nice. Set it up in your schedule to include some time in the gym.

If you do not like the traditional cardio machines, perhaps you **should join an intramural team for whatever sport you played** (or wished you had played) in high school. This is a great way to get some exercise, release some stress, meet some new people and have fun!

- **Take a PE Class!** I gained the Freshman 15 (more like 20) and was like "Oh Hell No, I'm not going out like this" I put myself into 1 PE Class for each semester so that I could get myself into the habit of working out. I always went to workout because I was getting a grade and it was an easy way to boost my GPA! I took Yoga (something I still practice today), Weight Training (where I learned how to work all the machines in the gym and use free weights), and aerobics. I got back in shape and created a health & wellness habit that I still keep up over 15 years later.

FIND yourSELF / STAY GROUNDED

College is awesome and it is fun to be FREE for the first time. Do not lose touch with your foundation or miss out on the opportunity get grounded. If you grew up in the church and believe in God, find a church home while you are in college so you can stay grounded.

If you do not have a strong spiritual practice or grow up with one, college can be a wonderful opportunity to explore spirituality and find out what works for you. Most campuses have resources for a variety of spiritual practices and I recommend developing your personal spiritual connection while in college, you will need it. Check into campus services and if there are none that work for you look into churches in the area. You may be able to get a ride from students or you may be able to call the church and get the shuttle to come and pick you up.

You will come up against a lot of pressures in college, having a strong spiritual connection and being grounded in your personal morals and values will make it easier to stay on track and finish school proud of who you are and what you did while there!

MONEY MATTERS

CREDIT CARDS

They lay in wait on campus just waiting for you to arrive. The credit card companies! They just love to entice you with campus packs, t–shirts, and all other sorts of free goodies "just for applying." Please be S.M.A.R.T., there is NO SUCH THING AS FREE MONEY! You do not need a credit card, and if you do, ask your parents to help you out.

My advice, **DO NOT GET A CREDIT CARD!** There is nothing worse than to graduate from college with "jacked–up credit." It can stop you from getting a good job, a good apartment, and even a student loan for the next year! You do not want to have to drop out of college because you bought a new wardrobe with the credit card you got freshman year. Buying stuff is not that important, just wait until you graduate and get a job!

BANKING

Do make sure you open a bank account if you do not have one. If you can, open your account with a bank that has branches both in your hometown and your school, it makes it easier for your family to get you money in an emergency!

GET YOUR HUSTLE ON

You may be lucky and not have to work while in college, but most people I know are on the hustle. If you have a job while in college, whether its work–study or something else, now is the time to start creating S.M.A.R.T. money habits. First of all make sure you **save at least 10% of what you make**. If you can master this skill of paying yourself first I promise when you get out of school you will have a head start on 90% of the country! Open a Savings Account and IMMEDIATELY put 10% of your check away (BTW You can add more if you like), and create a nest–egg/ emergency fund for yourself. I also recommend putting away another 5% as the "**FUN FUND!**" The Fun Fund is the perfect way to save for SPRING BREAK so that you have money for that new bikini or vacation fun.

S.M.A.R.T. Sistas know that life happens and are prepared when it does. Start being S.M.A.R.T. with your money now so that by the time you graduate it will be a habit and you will be great at managing your money when you start making the big bucks!

SAFETY

CAN SOMEBODY CALL SECURITY?!

HOW NOT TO GET YOUR STUFF STOLEN

It is weird having to share a room with a stranger and even worse living in a dorm with a bunch of them, but that is the reality of college life and it will start to prepare you for the real world.

Lock up your valuables! Your roommate may or may not be trustworthy, but what about her friends? You are not in control of who comes in and out of your room so I advise putting anything you do not want taken in a safe place or out of the line of sight. Do not leave your MP3 Player and or cell phone just laying out on your bed or night-stand. Get a little lock box or at a minimum a box that fastens and put them in it when you leave the room or are not using them.

If you have a laptop computer, do not just leave it on your desk unattended. You can get a laptop lock cable to secure it to the desk if you are studying somewhere and need to run to the bathroom or something. The best thing to do is shut it down and put it in a drawer, out of sight, or keep it on you.

When it comes to things like jewelry or anything that is extremely valuable or important it should be locked up. In some cases it may be best to leave it at home, but if you just have to have your grand-mother's pearls for your first semi–formal, invest in a small personal safe. The things in there should be irreplaceable and things you rarely use (valuable jewelry, social security card, birth certificate, passport, etc...). Keep your personal safe in an out of the way location. You do not want to call attention to it. People can get curious and it may become a target.

> *My college roommate stole my Identity! This was a young lady with whom I shared many great memories. When my mother got sick and died from cancer she comforted me. In fact she was the person who told me she died when I got home from class. We had the same major so we took classes and studied together. We shopped, shared boy stories and were great friends. She was even in my wedding! Then years later I went to volunteer and they ran my SSN for a background check and they asked me about XXXXXX person on my credit report. I was shocked! I never knew this because I had not been in the work force. It seemed she decided to take my SSN and opened up credit cards and did all sort of business using my identity. As roommates she had access to all sorts of information about me. I was very trusting. If anyone would have told me she would have done this I would have said it was not possible, but all I can say is "LOCK UP YOUR STUFF"*

Lock Your Door: Such a small thing, but Sista lock your room door whenever you leave. Yes it is a hassle, but do you really want to come back and find your stuff gone? Whether you are just doing laundry or going down to pick up the pizza, lock the door. Better to be safe than sorry.

MONEY MONEY MONEY: You do not need to keep a whole lot of money on you, but what you do have should be kept secure. I recommend keeping your cash on and/or close to you. Get one of those little pouches you attach to your key ring. You always carry your keys so keep your cash close too! If you want to have an emergency stash fine, this is another item that should be kept in your personal safe and only accessed in case of an emergency. Otherwise make sure you have a bank account and use your ATM card

LATE NIGHT, DATE NIGHT, RAPE NIGHT!

Sad to say that there are always stories of young women being raped on college campuses. Sometimes you can be lulled into a false sense of security, but college is no different than the real world. As a young Sista heading out into the world now is the time to learn how to protect yourself from the real predators out there.

LATE NIGHT

It is late, you had to stay in the computer lab working on a program or in the library researching a paper; now you have to get home, what do you do? If you happen to live right across from the library it is simple walk home, but on many campuses it is quite a trek from the academic buildings to the residence halls. Predators know this and unfortunately some will wait for the lone female walking on campus late at night or after dark. I want all my S.M.A.R.T. Sistas to be safe so here are a few tips

1. **Take a self–defense class.** Most campuses offer this on a regular basis. Take the time to learn how to protect yourself should you

find your safety compromised. It can happen anywhere so you want to be prepared

2. **Carry pepper–spray/mace:** I hope you never have to use it, but if your school allows it, keep a can on your key ring and keep it handy if you have no other option than to walk alone.[8]

3. **USE SAFE WALK/ SAFE RIDE/ SECURITY ESCORTS:** I cannot emphasize this enough. By now almost every campus offers some sort of service like this. It may take some planning ahead, but your safety is worth it. When you know you are about to wrap it up, put a call in to have an escort meet you and get you home safely. Keep the number in your phone and use it.

4. **Stay in a group:** There is safety in numbers so after a party or late–night event, walk home with a group of friends going to the same place! If 4 of you go to one dorm and the other has to go by herself, let her **stay the night or use an escort** to get the last girl home safely. It would be horrible to know that someone got snatched on a short walk from your dorm to hers.

---

[8] Most parties/clubs won't allow you to bring it in, so stash it somewhere before you go in and grab it when you go home.

DATE NIGHT

Date rape is all too common in college and in the real world. We often think it could never happen because we really like this guy and think he is cool. Take a moment; does ANYONE ever go out with someone they really think will rape them? When you are dating you are getting to know someone. In reality he could be a lunatic, so please be S.M.A.R.T. and keep yourself safe.

1. **Tell someone where you are going and with whom:** Make sure your friends know with whom you are going out and where you are going. That way if something does go screwy it will be that much easier to find you.

   If he is driving, text the make, model, and license plate of his ride to someone!

   This is yet another reason why the "secret affair" is not a good idea and why you need to have at least one good friend. Somebody should always know where you are!

2. **Always have a way home.** That may mean keeping enough in cab fare to take a taxi back to your dorm/apartment if things start to get weird. Have a cell phone or change for a pay phone handy too. I always tuck a $20 in my bra in case I have to leave my purse and phone behind.

3. **Date in public**: There are many reason I advise you to "keep the door open" and "be

seen in public." It is not all about maintaining a good reputation. It is a lot easier to run out of an open door than to unlock one and try to escape. Being in a public place will make it a lot harder for someone to attack you! You can snuggle in a movie theatre, just like you could watching a DVD in his room/apt. Most campuses have free or reduced price movies that make excellent date activities.

4. **Take it slow**: There is no rush, take the time to get to know him before being totally alone. Most of the time there are red flags to warn you of a potential attacker. Does he not respect your wishes to keep the door open? Does he get really angry if he does not get what he wants (think about if his order is messed up a restaurant or someone cuts him off in traffic, does he get bent out of shape or just go with the flow?)?

5. **Date in groups**: Double dates are a great way to have fun and keep it safe. See if he has a friend or invite your friend and her honey along to make it a group thing. Chances are they both are not crazy and if so, your girl will have your back!

6. **Be clear and be firm**: Do not play games and be wishy washy about getting intimate. You should know before you walk out the door how far you want things to go. You do not have to announce it at the beginning of the evening, but it is not cool to lead people on. There is NEVER AN EXCUSE for rape, but make sure it is very easy for him to un-

derstand that you do not want to have sex. If you are naked and helped him put on a condom, but "change your mind" at the last minute he will still be wrong if he does not stop, but why make it that hard. You should know beforehand if you are ready for the next step or not. If you are not sure, you are not ready, it is that simple.

Wrapping It Up

I will leave you with this. College should one the best times of your life. It is the perfect mixture of freedom from your parent's rules and regulations without ALL the responsibility of being totally on your own. Your room and board is covered, your food is paid for (if you have a great meal plan) yet you get to set your own hours and make all the decisions about what you do with your time.

The thing is, with freedom comes responsibility. No one is going to look over your shoulder to make sure you study, eat right, and make S.M.A.R.T. decisions. At the end of the semester your grades, appearance and state of mind will reflect the choices you make and you will have to live with the consequences. Some people will be on academic probation, others will be on the Dean's List. Some will have lots of friends others will be lonely. You have the power to create an awesome college experience or look back with regrets and disappointments. I hope this guide gave you some insights and that you will reference it often. If there is ANYTHING you do not see covered in here, please visit us online at **www.SmartSistasWin.com** and visit the FORUMS. You can ask questions about anything and I or one of the other S.M.A.R.T. Sistas will be sure to answer. Also find a mentor or an older woman in your life that you admire and ask her about her collegiate experience. Big Sistas love to look out for our Little Sistas so use us! Have fun and be S.M.A.R.T.!

Kania Kennedy, the S.M.A.R.T. Sista is a graduate of Duke University holds a Bachelor's of Science, in Electrical & Computer Engineering, is a member of Delta Sigma Theta Sorority, Inc, Life Coach, and a Business Owner. Kania started the Smart Sistas project as a way to share the wisdom of her mother and her life experiences with Sistas of all ages! She is committed to helping Young Sistas transition into womanhood and Grown Sistas live the fabulous life! She currently resides in Chicago, IL and is CEO, and founder of Diva Dance.

Kania is available for Motivational, Educational, Inspirational, and Transformational Speaking Engagements. You may reach Kania at www.TheSmartSista.com or hello@TheSmartSista.com

Photo Courtesy of Deluan Fuller Photography

Made in the USA
Monee, IL
03 April 2021